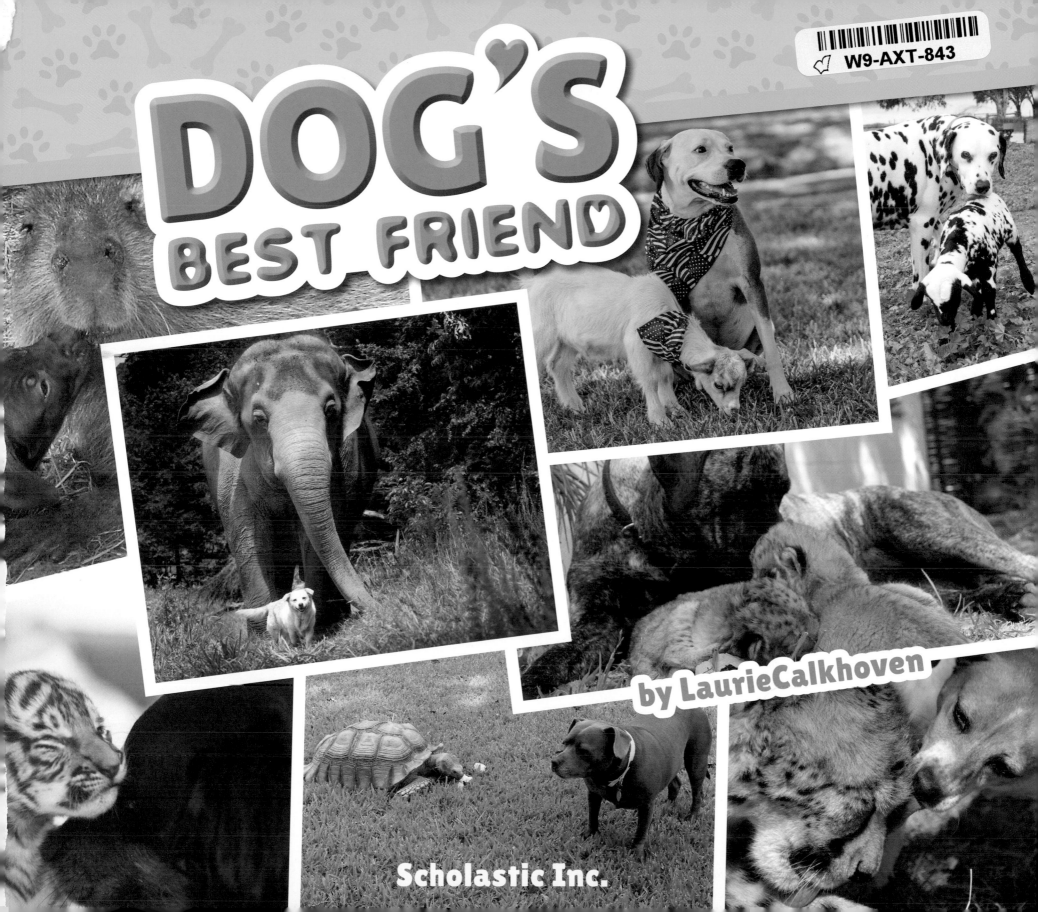

DOG'S BEST FRIEND

by LaurieCalkhoven

Scholastic Inc.

ISBN 978-1-338-22716-1

10 9 8 7 6 5 4 3 2 1   18 19 20 21 22
Printed in China   68

First edition, September 2018

Book design by Jessica Meltzer
Photo research by Emily Teresa

INTRODUCTION

Dogs and humans have been best friends for thousands of years. Dogs have walked at hunters' sides, protected farmers' herds, and have even gone to war to fight alongside and protect their human companions. But mostly dogs have loved us and been our best friends. So maybe it shouldn't surprise us that dogs can also be best friends with some pretty unlikely creatures, like the big cats of Africa and India, dolphins, owls, and even elephants!

Read on to learn about the pooches that rescued a baby kangaroo, taught a monkey how to be a member of a monkey family, and loved baby animals that were rejected by their mothers.

Friendship comes in all different shapes and sizes. All of the friendships in this book are unique, but they all begin with a friendly, loving dog.

3

DOGS and CHEETAHS

Who said dogs and cats can't get along? At zoos and wildlife parks around the country, dogs and cheetahs are living together and loving it. In fact, some cheetahs even prefer to live with their canine companions rather than alone.

Cheetahs, which can run as fast as 70 miles per hour, are the fastest land animals on Earth. In the wild they're always on the lookout for **predators**, and their natural instinct isn't to fight–it's to run. In a zoo, cheetahs are provided opportunities to thrive, which sometimes involves providing them a companion.

That's where dogs and puppies come in. Dogs are brave, smart, and friendly, and, more importantly, they trust humans. Cheetah cubs are often paired with puppies from a very young age. Puppies not only like to play, much like cheetah cubs, but having a dog buddy also teaches cheetahs that humans can be trusted.

The very first cheetah/dog pairing occurred at the San Diego Zoo in 1980. Arusha, a male cheetah, was paired with a golden retriever named Anna. Arusha had been rejected by his mother at another zoo and had to be raised by hand. When he arrived in San Diego, zookeepers realized that he needed a friend. So they got him a dog: Anna.

When Arusha hissed and swatted at the pup, Anna wasn't afraid, and she showed him who was boss. They soon became best friends. They snuggled at night, groomed each other, and played during the day.

Anna, a Golden Retriever, became Arusha's companion when he arrived at the San Diego Zoo.

Now, because of that first friendship between Anna and Arusha, there are many dog and cheetah buddies at zoos and wildlife parks across the country.

Dogs are helping cheetahs in the wild, too. In southern Africa, where most wild cheetahs live, **livestock** was easy **prey** for hungry cheetahs. Farmers would shoot the wild cats to protect their herds. That's where dogs came in. The Cheetah Conservation Fund raised Anatolian shepherd dogs, which were originally **bred** in Turkey to protect livestock from wolves and bears, and gave them to farmers to guard their cows, goats, and sheep. The big dogs scare away the wild cats. Farmers are happy, and the cheetahs remain free to hunt another day.

BEST FRIENDS FOREVER

Arusha hissed and swatted at Anna at first, but the pair quickly became best friends.

EDEN and CHLOE
Cheetah Experience, Bloemfontein, South Africa

AMANI and WINDSPEAR
Dallas Zoo, Dallas, Texas

BRAVO and CJ
Cincinnati Zoo, Cincinnati, Ohio

MTANI and KASI
Busch Gardens, Tampa Bay, Florida

BLAKELY the AUSTRALIAN SHEPHERD and HIS TIGER CUBS

If you think dogs and cheetahs are a strange combination, what about dogs and tigers?

At the Cincinnati Zoo in Ohio, three rare Malayan tiger cubs—Chira, Batari, and Izzy—were ignored by their mother shortly after their birth in February 2017. There are fewer than 500 wild Malayan tigers, which live in Malaysia and southern Thailand, left in the world. Zoo workers knew how important these cubs were, and stepped in to raise them by hand. But the tigers needed more than humans to help them feel safe and happy. That's where Blakely the Australian shepherd came in.

Australian shepherds, which were actually developed in the United States and not in Australia, are smart, loyal dogs. The zoo thought Blakely would be a great nanny for the tiger cubs. Luckily, they were right.

Blakely did more than snuggle with the cubs. He played with them and let them know with strong but gentle nudges when they were being too rough. Spending time with Blakely prepared the tiger cubs to join the rest of the big cats in the zoo's Cat Canyon.

This wasn't Blakely's first time playing nanny to newborns. He's also cuddled with cheetahs, an ocelot, a takin, a warthog, wallabies, skunks, and even bat-eared foxes!

What happened when a tiger rejected her cubs? Blakely became their nanny!

BETH the RHODESIAN RIDGEBACK and HER LION CUBS

A long time ago, Rhodesian ridgeback dogs helped African hunters go after big cats like lions. Bull mastiffs, another large-dog breed, were raised to act as guard dogs for **gamekeepers**. So you might expect Beth, a 100-pound mastiff and Rhodesian ridgeback mix, to hunt big cats or at least keep them at bay.

But that's not what Beth wants to do at all. Beth lives on a 1,000-acre **game reserve** in South Africa, surrounded by zebras, giraffes, warthogs, and the second-biggest cats in the world—lions.

Lions once roamed Africa, Asia, and Europe. Today you can only find them in central and southern Africa and in India's Gir Forest. Just one out of 10 lion cubs survives its first year in the

Beth loved to run and play with lion cubs.

wild, so cubs born on the game reserve are raised until they are strong enough to be released to wildlife reserves or into the African bush.

Lions, unlike other wild cats, are social animals. They live in groups called **prides**. Dogs are social animals, too, and that's where Beth came in. Beth loved to run and play with the reserve's lion cubs. But she wasn't just another fuzzy creature to play with; Beth also acted like a mom, licking the cubs clean like any lion mother would do.

Once the lions got to be about a year old, they were too strong and too big for Beth to play with without fear of getting hurt. But Beth didn't seem to mind. She went on to "mother" several kittens and baby baboons!

Thanks to Beth's care and attention, at least five lion clubs have been released into the bush and onto other game reserves.

BEST FRIENDS FOREVER

Sometimes a lion just needs to snuggle.

MISCHKA the BERNESE MOUNTAIN DOG and HER FERRET

There are many odd couples in this book, but the strangest-friendship award may belong to Mischka, a 90-pound Bernese mountain dog, and her friend Jerry, a ferret that is about 40 times smaller!

Bernese mountain dogs were first bred in the mountains of Switzerland. These gentle giants are calm and playful, but they also like to work. In the old days they pulled small wagons filled with people or crops. A dog like Mischka can pull up to 10 times its body weight.

One day, Mischka was in the front yard when one of her neighbors walked by with her pet ferret, Jerry, on a leash. The two very different creatures sniffed each other carefully, and then they started to play.

Mischka and Jerry share their toys!

BEST FRIENDS FOREVER

Mischka is 40 times bigger than Jerry, but that doesn't stop them from being best friends.

Ferrets, which are related to weasels, otters, and badgers, are tame and playful, but they aren't known for making friends with other **species**. Jerry made an exception for Mischka.

The next day, when Mischka heard the bell on Jerry's collar, she went to the front door and started to bark. Every day during Jerry's walk, Mischka goes outside for a visit. They even have regular play dates.

The big dog is always gentle with her little friend, and Jerry loves snuggling in Mischka's fur. They may be an odd couple, but they don't seem to mind one bit!

SOPHIE the SPRINGER SPANIEL and BRAMBLE the OWL

Sophie, a springer spaniel, has special privileges at a bird-prey conservation center in Cornwall, England. She gets to live in the house with her owner, Sharon Bindon.

In the wild, owls prey on small **mammals** like Sophie, so the spaniel had never gotten to meet one of the birds close up. Then Bramble the Eurasian eagle **owlet** showed up. Eurasian eagle owls are one of the largest species of owl in the world, but Bramble was just two weeks old. The bird's feathers hadn't grown in yet (that takes about seven weeks) and she wasn't able to fly. Bramble wouldn't survive in the center's **aviary**, so the owlet was brought into the house.

Spaniels were originally hunting dogs, but Sophie didn't try to hunt Bramble. She wanted to be the owlet's mom! Sophie licked and cuddled the little bird until Bramble started to follow her everywhere.

Soon, Bramble was big enough and strong enough to fly and to join the other birds in the aviary, but she and Sophie remained good friends. Every day before taking flight, Bramble flew down to visit Sophie. Sophie licked Bramble's beak, and Bramble "beaked" Sophie in return.

BEST FRIENDS FOREVER

Bramble was just two weeks old and feather-less when she met Sophie. Sophie licked and cuddled the owlet to make her feel safe.

ROO the CHIHUAHUA and HER SILKIE CHICKEN

Roo, a Chihuahua dog that was born without his two front legs, was found in a ditch on the side of the road. Penny is a silkie chicken that was rescued from an animal testing facility. It's no wonder that when the two rescue animals wound up living in the same home, they became the best of friends.

Penny doesn't look like any chicken you've ever seen. Penny is a silkie, a kind of chicken that looks more like a soft, furry cloud than a chicken. If not for her little beak, you'd never know what she was. Silkies, which originally came from China, have blue earlobes and black skin hidden under their white feathers.

When Penny's owner brought little Roo home, Penny immediately checked him out. When Roo fell asleep, Penny climbed on top of him like he was her egg. They've been side by side ever since!

Two rescue animals—the best of friends.

Roo has a special wheelchair that allows him to run around at top speed. The pair plays together, naps together, and even goes to work at an animal hospital with their owner. They love to greet their guests—human or otherwise!

Sometimes Roo and Penny take walks together.

And sometimes they just cuddle.

JOKER the MUTT and the DOLPHINS

Have you ever wanted to spend a day at the beach? A mixed-breed dog named Joker slips out of his family's home in Israel every day to go to the beach. More specifically, he visits a beach called Dolphin Reef in the Red Sea.

Dolphin Reef is a place where bottlenose dolphins and other animals like cats, chickens, and peacocks live and sometimes "visit" with humans. One day, Joker wandered onto the beach. He sat on the pier and watched the dolphins playing in the water. Joker started going back day after day to watch the dolphins jump and play.

One time, Joker jumped right into the water to join in the fun! The dolphins were curious about the hairy little creature, so they played along.

They had so much fun that the next time Joker visited and sat on the pier, the dolphins

The dolphins were having so much fun that Joker decided to join them.

clicked and whistled to get his attention. It must have been an invitation, because the curious dog jumped in once again and kept coming back.

Joker lives a few miles away and walks over to Dolphin Reef every day. But a day of playing in the water must tire him out. When it's time for him to go home, he waits in the parking lot for one of the Dolphin Reef's employees. When someone heads to his or her car, Joker tags along and jumps in for a ride home!

Come on in, the water's fine!

THE DACHSHUND/PIT BULL PUPPIES and THEIR CAPYBARA

Imagine the surprise at the Rocky Ridge Refuge in Midway, Arkansas, when they learned that Cheesecake, their capybara, had hidden talents. Capybaras, from Central and South America, are the world's largest rodent. They can grow to be as big as four feet long and look like giant guinea pigs. Capybaras are social animals—they like to be in groups—but no one knew those groups included puppies!

One day, seven abandoned dachshund/pit bull-mix puppies arrived at the refuge. The owner, Janice Wolf, didn't have an open pen available for the tiny puppies to keep them safe from the other dogs, tortoises, deer, birds, and rabbits that were already on the property. So she put them in Cheesecake's heated pen and hoped for the best.

Before long, the capybara had adopted the little guys. Cheesecake was nervous around humans, but she loved the puppies. She played with them all day and let them sleep next to her at night.

The puppies have since been adopted from the refuge. But don't worry about Cheesecake. She went on to adopt more litters of puppies, including Great Pyrenees mixes and American bulldog mixes.

No doubt Cheesecake will be acting as a puppy nanny for a long time to come!

Cheesecake adopted many litters of puppies, but these were her first.

BEST FRIENDS FOREVER

WINSTON the LABRADOR RETRIEVER and KAMMER the CHAMELEON

Most of the animal friendships in this book, as strange and unusual as they are, are between two different types of mammals, or between a mammal and a bird. But what happens when a dog (mammal) meets a chameleon (reptile)? In the case of Winston, the yellow lab, and Kammer, the chameleon, it was love at first sight.

Chameleons, a kind of lizard, have eyes that can move independently of each other, skin that changes color, and super-fast tongues that fold up like an accordion in their mouths.

Kammer isn't the first chameleon to enter Winston's life. His owner also has a chameleon named Geoffrey. The two creatures tolerated each other, but when Kammer joined the household, everything changed. The dog and the chameleon checked each other out, and a friendship was quickly born.

Sometimes Winston and Kammer share a meal.

BEST FRIENDS FOREVER

Winston and Kammer love to snuggle.

The two friends are hardly ever apart. They eat their meals out of matching bowls, play in the garden together, and even sleep together.

If fact, Kammer often nods off while resting on top of Winton's head. Winston doesn't mind. After all, that's what friends are for.

JASMINE the GREYHOUND and HER MENAGERIE

In Warwickshire, England, police officers heard strange noises coming from a garden shed one day. They opened the shed to find a small greyhound dog, shivering and half-starved. The dog had been abused. It was afraid of humans and whimpered when it heard loud noises.

Greyhounds, the second-fastest land animal (only cheetahs are faster), are often used as racing dogs. When they start to lose races, some owners abandon the dogs. That might have been what happened to this poor dog.

The police took the dog to a nearby wildlife sanctuary. The people there named her Jasmine and nursed her back to health. After several weeks of careful treatment and lots of love, Jasmine was strong and healthy. She also learned to trust humans again.

The sanctuary wanted to find a nice family to take Jasmine in, but the dog had other ideas. Every time someone brought a new animal to the sanctuary, Jasmine gave the creature a gentle lick to say hello.

Greyhounds are bred to chase rabbits, but Jasmine had other ideas.

It's not just rabbits she liked to cuddle. Fawns got their share of attention, too.

She made friends with fox and badger cubs. She greeted swans and hedgehogs. She let a bird perch on her nose and acted like a shepherd herding chicks. Jasmine even licked rabbits, an animal that greyhounds are bred to chase. And when newborn puppies turned up in a box, Jasmine tucked them close to her as if they were her own.

All of the animals Jasmine "mothered" became lively and strong. One fox cub, Roxy, became so attached to Jasmine that she stayed on at the sanctuary instead of being released back into the wild.

Jasmine and Roxy often took walks together, but there were other animals that needed the

greyhound's help. One was a tiny fawn. Hikers had found the baby deer in the woods and knew that something was wrong. They took her to a **veterinarian** who said there was no hope for her. But the hikers didn't give up. They brought the fawn to the wildlife sanctuary and that's when Jasmine took over.

When Bramble the fawn wasn't being bottle-fed, Jasmine licked her clean and snuggled next to her to keep her warm. Bramble got stronger and stronger, and before long she and Jasmine were taking walks together, too.

Even when Bramble got too big for the house and moved to the barn, Jasmine went to visit her every day. They rubbed their cheeks together and Jasmine always gave Bramble a lick.

Jasmine passed away in 2011, but not before she had cared for five fox cubs, four badger cubs, fifteen chicks, eight guinea pigs, two stray puppies, fifteen rabbits, and one very lucky deer!

The animals Jasmine "mothered" became lively and strong.

LADY the POODLE and DILLIE the DEER

♥

Dillie, a white-tailed deer, was born almost completely blind and was abandoned by her mother. The three-day-old fawn couldn't eat or even stand. She wouldn't have survived long if a veterinarian hadn't stepped in and brought the baby deer home.

There were already a number of other animals living in the vet's home, including a poodle named Lady. Lady licked the frightened and hungry deer all over. She snuggled with Dillie every day until the deer was strong enough to stand and eat on her own.

Before long, Dillie was up and running. After spending so much time with Lady, she seemed to think she was a dog, too! Following Lady's lead, Dillie was soon housebroken. She also slept in her owners' bed, just like Lady. When she got too big for that, Dillie took over a guest room. Lady often visited Dillie at naptime so the two animals could curl up together.

Dillie and Lady played games like tug-of-war with stuffed animals, and Lady even taught Dillie how to reach onto high shelves to snag treats for the two of them to share! Dillie eats a lot of fresh hay and salads, but her favorite food is ice cream. For an extra-special treat, she'll get roses!

BEST FRIENDS FOREVER

Lady and Dillie napped together, at least when they weren't playing with stuffed animals!

KATJINGA the RHODESIAN RIDGEBACK and HER PIGLET

If you've ever seen a Rhodesian ridgeback dog, you know that they're big. They can also be fierce. So fierce that years ago, people in Africa used them to help hunt lions and other big game. But Katjinga, a Rhodesian ridgeback living in Germany, is the opposite of fierce. She's a gentle farm dog that adopted a newborn Vietnamese potbellied pig.

Katjinga's owner found the newborn piglet (now named Paulinchen) alone and shivering on his farm. The piglet had been left by her mother, perhaps because the mother thought the baby was too small to survive.

The farmer brought the tiny piglet home and set her down near Katjinga. The big dog was a mother herself and immediately started treating Paulinchen like one of her puppies. Katjinga licked the little piglet all over to clean her, and then snuggled up next to her to keep her warm.

Katjinga treated Paulinchen just like one of her puppies.

The dog and her piglet had a friendship that lasted forever.

Both the farmer and Katjinga took care of Paulinchen until she was strong enough to rejoin her family. But Paulinchen never forgot Katjinga.

Every time she saw the big, gentle dog around the farm she ran over to say hello. Some friendships really do last forever.

ZOE the DALMATION and HER LITTLE SPOTTED LAMB

When you think about Dalmatians, you might think about a firehouse dog. That's because Dalmatians were originally bred to get along with horses. Dalmatians used to run alongside horse-drawn fire trucks and keep the horses calm while firefighters put out the blaze.

One thing you probably don't associate with Dalmatians is sheep! But Zoe, a Dalmatian living in Australia, adopted a spotted lamb of her very own.

When the lamb, now named Lambie, was born, her mother pushed her away. Lambie's owners knew they would have to raise the lamb by hand if she was going to survive. That's when Zoe stepped in. Perhaps she was drawn to the newborn's smell, or maybe she just liked the little lamb's black spots. Zoe immediately began to nuzzle Lambie and lick her clean.

Zoe stepped in when Lambie's mother pushed her away.

A lamb needs two things to survive—food and a flock. Zoe wasn't able to feed her new friend, but she was always nearby when Lambie had her bottle. The dog became the little lamb's flock.

Lambie followed Zoe around the barnyard, played with her and the other dogs, and even slept in Zoe's dog kennel. The abandoned lamb grew to be strong and healthy, all because of her attachment to a spotted dog.

Lambie grew strong with Zoe's loving help.

PIPER the PIT BULL and HER GOAT KID

When goats deliver triplets, one of the babies usually doesn't survive. And that's exactly what was about to happen when a first-time goat mother gave birth to three babies, called kids. The first of the three kids wasn't moving, and the mother ran to the other side of the pen to give birth to her next two babies.

The kid, now called Goat Puppy or GP for short, was going to have to be raised by hand if he was going to survive. GP's owner rushed him inside the house and laid him down on a heating pad.

Piper, a pit bull mix living in the house, immediately stepped in to act as a mother to the kid. Pit bull dogs have a reputation for being aggressive, but that's just a myth. Most pit bulls love people and other animals, and they really love to cuddle. Piper licked GP all over until he started to move, and she rarely left his side. She licked GP's chin clean after he had been fed with a bottle, and curled up around him while he slept. GP even went on walks with Piper, attached to a leash just like his adopted mom.

When GP hurt his leg and needed surgery, Piper was right there in the operating room. Afterward, she gently watched over her little kid until he was able to run and play again.

Wherever Piper goes, GP follows. And if Piper gets too far away, GP bleats to let his dog mom know it's time to come back.

BEST FRIENDS FOREVER

Wherever Piper went, Goat Puppy followed. That's just what friends do.

FREDDIE and PERCY, the JACK RUSSELL TERRIERS, and a SHETLAND PONY

Have you ever seen a dog on horseback? Freddie, a Jack Russell terrier living in England, was watching Daisy, a Shetland pony, giving children rides when he decided he wanted a ride, too. So he raced across the **paddock** and jumped right onto Daisy's back!

Luckily, Daisy didn't mind. She treated the dog just like any other rider. After that, Freddie started going on two or three rides a day.

It didn't stop there. Freddie had a Jack Russell friend named Percy, and Percy wanted to do everything Freddie did. One day when Freddie was riding Daisy, Percy jumped right up next to him!

After that, Percy became a regular horseback rider. The dogs mostly take turns, but sometimes they go for rides together. They also enjoy going for rides in a little cart that Daisy pulls.

Local children love to watch and cheer for the dogs and their pony friend.

Freddie and Percy rode Daisy every chance they got. Luckily, Daisy didn't mind!

REX the POINTER MIX and the KANGAROO

Rex, a pointer mix living in Australia, had just returned from a walk when he tried to draw his owner's attention to a kangaroo that had been killed by a car. His owner ignored him, but then Rex picked up something in his mouth and gently dropped it at his owner's feet.

Rex had saved a baby kangaroo, called a **joey**, that was still in its mother's pouch. Joeys are about the size of a lima bean when they're born. Unable to survive outside, they stay in their mothers' pouches for as long as eight months before stepping out into the world. If not for Rex, the joey would not have survived.

Rex immediately started nuzzling and caring for the joey, and the joey snuggled right up to Rex.

Rex and Rex Jr. side by side.

Dog and joey stayed at each other's sides until the baby kangaroo, nicknamed Rex Jr., was taken to a wildlife sanctuary where it was hand raised until it was big enough and strong enough to be released into the wild.

Rex visited the sanctuary a few weeks later, and he and his joey immediately recognized each other. Perhaps they'll find each other again one day when Rex Jr. is released back into the wild.

BEST FRIENDS FOREVER

Will dog and kangaroo find each other again when Rex Jr. is released into the wild?

PITTY the PIT BULL, and KITTY the KITTEN

Pit bulls have a bad reputation, but the truth is that most of them are sweethearts. Pitty, a stray dog, is a perfect example of that. When Pitty was found on the side of a road in Texas, she had recently given birth to a litter of puppies. The puppies were nowhere near, but that didn't stop this sweet dog from being a mother. A tiny kitten, one so young its eyes weren't yet open, was found with the dog, drinking her milk!

The dog, now named Pitty, was thin and hungry, but she still fed and licked the kitten. When the staff at an animal hospital separated them, Pitty howled as if her heart was broken.

Sadly, Kitty had a birth defect and passed away, but a family heard about the loving dog and adopted her. Pitty entered a family of three cats and two other dogs. At first she seemed to be looking for Kitty and cried when she didn't find her. Then she got the chance to mother another stray kitten.

Kitty II was found in a mud puddle one stormy night. Pitty stood by when the kitten was brought into the house. For the next two weeks she watched over the kitten, licking and cuddling the new baby. Today, they're the best of friends!

Pitty and Kitty.

DOLLY the PIT BULL and SHELDON the TORTOISE

Have you heard the story about the tortoise and the hare? How about the tortoise and the pit bull?

Dolly the pit bull and Sheldon the tortoise were both adopted from an animal shelter. Dolly's owners expected her to become BFFs with their other dog, Daisy, but Dolly was much more interested in Sheldon the tortoise.

At first Sheldon pulled his head and legs into his shell when Dolly got too close. Then they circled each other for a while, and finally they started to play.

Sheldon is a sulcata tortoise, a species that normally lives on the southern edge of the Sahara desert in Africa. Sulcatas are the third-largest species of tortoise in the world (the Galápagos and Aldabra giant tortoises are both larger).

They can live to be 100 years old and weigh up to 200 pounds!

Sheldon the tortoise was scared at first, but Dolly won him over.

For all that weight, Sheldon is a surprisingly fast runner. He chases after Dolly, and she runs away only to come back again. Sometimes this game of tag goes on for hours. Dolly has also tried to get Sheldon interested in her favorite red ball, but so far Sheldon doesn't have any interest in playing fetch!

BEST FRIENDS FOREVER

Dolly and Sheldon love to play tag, but Sheldon won't play fetch!

ROSCOE the BLUETICK HOUND and SURYIA the ORANGUTAN

It was just another ordinary day for Suryia the orangutan, hitching a ride on the back of an elephant named Bubbles. The two friends both lived on an **endangered** species preserve in South Carolina and were heading to the river for a swim. That's when they spotted a bluetick coonhound on the riverbank.

Blueticks are smart, friendly dogs. Orangutans, which usually live in the rain forests on the Pacific islands of Sumatra and Borneo, spend most of their lives up in the trees. So dogs and orangutans don't often meet and make friends.

But for some reason that day, Suryia hopped off Bubbles and ran over to the dog, which was later named Roscoe. Suryia said hello orangutan style—with a big, hairy hug. Roscoe didn't mind, and before long the unlikely pair were playing together like long-lost friends.

When it was time for Suryia and Bubbles to go home, Roscoe tagged along and made himself at home. When no one claimed the dog, Roscoe became an official member of the wildlife preserve. Soon, he and Suryia were doing everything together—napping, eating, swimming, playing, and even going for joint rides on Bubbles!

Theirs may be an unlikely friendship, but they don't care one bit.

Roscoe and Suryia do everything together. They even make the same faces!

BELLA the MUTT and TARRA the ELEPHANT

The Elephant Sanctuary in Hohenwald, Tennessee, must have looked like a nice place to live to a stray dog. The strays that wandered in there mostly ignored the elephants, and the elephants ignored them, too. Then a mutt, later named Bella, showed up, took one look at Tarra, an Asian elephant, and a lifelong friendship was born.

Tarra was captured in Burma (today called Myanmar) in 1974 and brought to the United States when she was just six months old. After twenty years of working in circuses and zoos, she became the first resident of the Elephant Sanctuary, in 1995. Elephants are social animals. They live in herds and form strong friendships. Those friendships just don't often extend to dogs!

Shortly after Bella the mutt arrived at the sanctuary in 2003, the pair became best friends. Bella loved Tarra and Tarra loved her back. That became really clear when Bella was injured. She couldn't move her legs or wag her tail. For three weeks she had to stay motionless in the sanctuary's office. Instead of roaming free on the land's 2,700 acres, Tarra stood beside the gate day after day and waited for her friend to feel better.

When the best buds were finally reunited, Tarra trumpeted with joy and stamped her feet while Bella practically danced with excitement. They were inseparable for the rest of Bella's life. They played together, ate together, and had sleepovers in the barn.

When Bella died in 2011, the rest of the elephants at the sanctuary knew how sad Tarra was. They were extra nice to her and even gave her portions of their food.

That's because elephants, like people and dogs, love and take care of their friends.

Bella and Tarra took one look at each other and became best friends forever!

GLOSSARY

Aviary: An enclosure or pen for birds, usually with netting overhead to keep them from flying away.

Breed: To make an animal have babies in a controlled way. Animals born in zoos are **bred** in captivity.

Endangered: In danger of dying out and disappearing in the natural world.

Game: Wild animals and birds. Game is often watched over by **gamekeepers** who live on game **reserves**.

Joey: A baby kangaroo.

Livestock: Animals kept or raised, especially farm animals.

Mammal: Warm-blooded animals that nourish their young with milk. Humans and dogs are both types of mammals.

Menagerie: A collection of animals.

Owlet: A baby owl.

Paddock: An enclosed area where animals eat grass and exercise.

Predator: An animal that hunts and eats other animals.

Prey: An animal that is hunted by another animal for food.

Pride: A group of lions.

Species: A category of living things that are alike in many ways. Dogs, whose species name is *Canis familiaris*, are one species. Humans, or *Homo sapiens*, are another.

Veterinarian: A doctor who specializes in treating animals.